Contents

DEEP TROUBLE

Like most people, you probably enjoy swimming or surfing in beautiful blue oceans. But, have you ever wondered what could be lurking under those sparkling waves? Some sand and seaweed, maybe some little fish like Nemo and his friends? Perhaps, but sometimes, there's a lot more! There's a world of deadly creatures down there … hopefully you won't be their next meal!

When it comes to dangerous fish, most people have heard of Jaws, but the fearsome great white isn't the only ocean dweller we should be afraid of. Seawater covers more than two-thirds of Earth's surface, so just imagine the number of deadly creatures in the dark depths of the sea.

Some sea creatures bite, some sting, and others … well, you will just have to see for yourself! The sea creatures in this book were ranked according to their aggression; their dangerous effects on human beings; and their deceiving appearances. As you swim through this book, ask yourself this question:

Deadliest Sea Creatures

Jack Booth

Series Editor
Jeffrey D. Wilhelm

Much thought, debate, and research went into choosing and ranking the 10 items in each book in this series. We realize that everyone has his or her own opinion of what is most significant, revolutionary, amazing, deadly, and so on. As you read, you may agree with our choices, or you may be surprised — and that's the way it should be!

an imprint of

SCHOLASTIC

www.scholastic.com/librarypublishing

A Rubicon book published in association with Scholastic Inc.

Ru'bĭcon © 2007 Rubicon Publishing Inc.
www.rubiconpublishing.com

 is a trademark of The 10 Books

Associate Publishers: Kim Koh, Miriam Bardswich
Project Editor: Amy Land
Editor: Amy Land
Creative Director: Jennifer Drew
Project Manager/Designer: Jeanette MacLean
Graphic Designer: Jeanette MacLean

The publisher gratefully acknowledges the following for permission to reprint copyrighted material in this book.

Every reasonable effort has been made to trace the owners of copyrighted material and to make due acknowledgment. Any errors or omissions drawn to our attention will be gladly rectified in future editions.

"Attacked by a Barracuda" by Paul Herring. Used with permission.

"Sea lion plucks Alaska fisherman off boat" (excerpt) by Peter Porco from the *Anchorage Daily News*. Used with permission.

"Girl dies after box jellyfish sting," from the Australian Associated Press. Used with permission.

Cover image: Great white shark–© SeaPics.com

Library and Archives Canada Cataloguing in Publication

Booth, Jack, 1946-
      The 10 deadliest sea creatures / Jack Booth.

Includes index.
ISBN 978-1-55448-482-9

      1. Readers (Elementary) 2. Readers—Marine animals. I. Title.
II. Title: Ten deadliest sea creatures.

PE1117.B6612245 2007   428.6   C2007-900578-0

1 2 3 4 5 6 7 8 9 10   10   16 15 14 13 12 11 10 09 08 07

Printed in Singapore

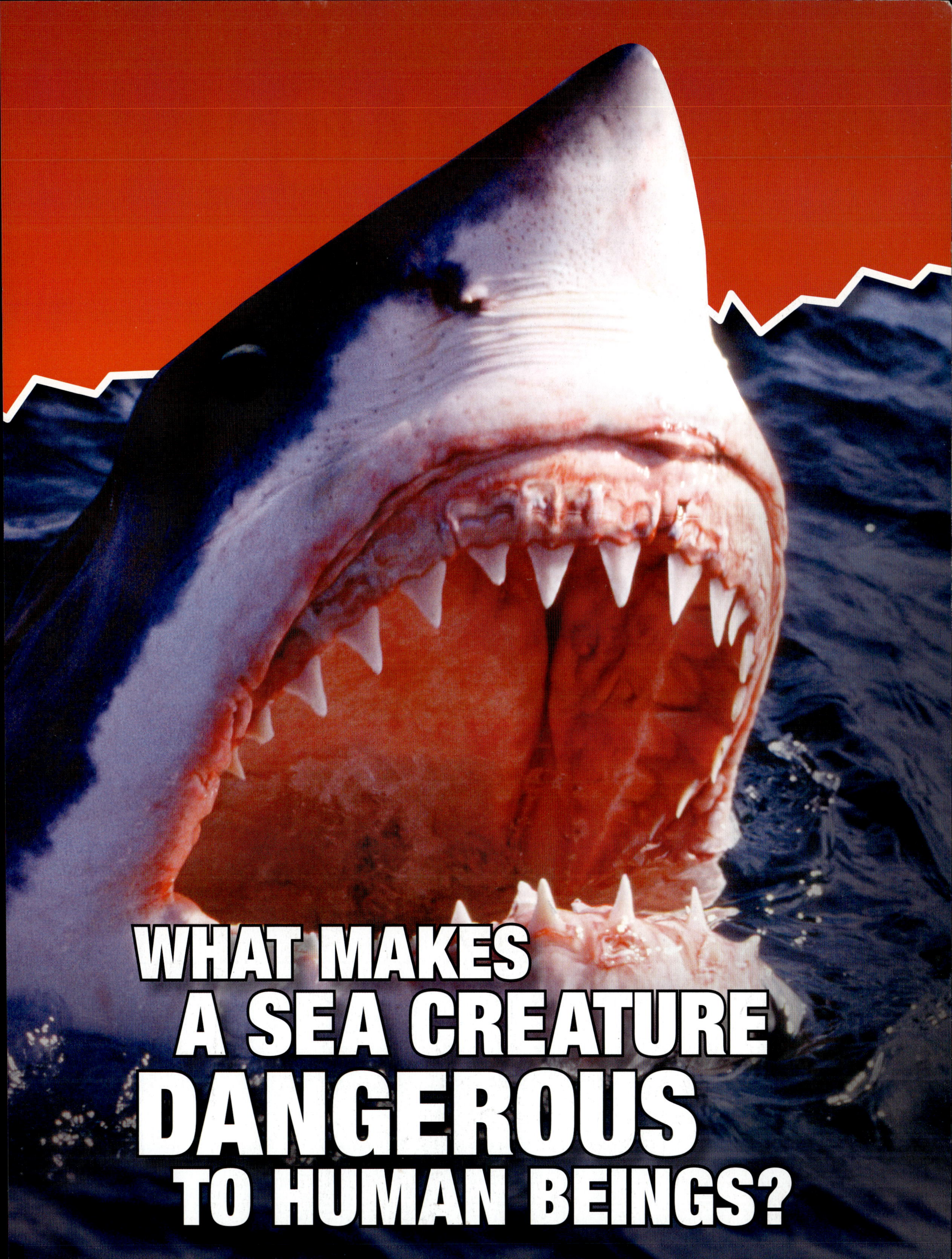

WHAT MAKES
A SEA CREATURE
DANGEROUS
TO HUMAN BEINGS?

SEA LION

The sea lion got its name from the roaring sound it makes.

You might think they look cute, cuddly, and even playful, but watch it! Sea lions are the original sea hooligans — and you'd better stay off their turf! They are extremely territorial. They don't want any other animals in their habitats, including you!

Sea lion attacks on people are much more common than you think! And if you think you can take one on, think again! This heavyweight can tip the scales at over 2,000 pounds.

Turn the page for more reasons why the mighty sea lion weighs in at #10 on our list of deadliest sea creatures ...

Did you expect to find the sea lion on a list of dangerous sea creatures? Explain your answer.

SEA LION

HOME SWEET HOME

Sea lions can be found along the west coast of North America, from British Columbia to the southern tip of California and Mexico. Some types of sea lions can also be found in Alaska, Japan, and Australia.

IF LOOKS COULD KILL

Males may reach 6.5 feet in length. Females can be up to 6 feet. California sea lions have 34 to 38 teeth: large canine teeth, smaller incisors, and cone-shaped cheek teeth.

Quick Fact

In April 2007, a sea lion attacked a 13-year-old girl in Australia. The girl was surfing behind a speedboat as the sea lion jumped out of the water. The sea creature then used its mouth to grab the girl's head!

FOOD FOR THOUGHT

Sea lions eat fish, squid, crabs, and clams. Some sea lions also eat penguins. They swallow most of their food whole. They toss their food up and around in their mouths and swallow it down headfirst.

BUT WHAT DOES IT DO?

A sea lion's sleek body is perfect for deep diving. Sea lions can dive as deep as 600 feet in search of tasty fish and squid. Sea lions are fast swimmers. In short bursts, they can swim over 25 mph. Sea lions are mammals that breathe air so they can't stay underwater for a long time. Sea lions are known to be very moody. When they feel intimidated by people, they can bite them with their sharp teeth.

If a sea lion barks, watch out! It's giving you a warning!

Quick Fact

Sea lions are most aggressive during the breeding season. Males establish dominance by open-mouth threats and vocalizing, pushing, and shoving.

? How do human beings display dominant behaviors when they are in a group?

10   9   8   7   6

Sea lion plucks Alaska fisherman off boat

A newspaper article from *Anchorage Daily News*, March 11, 2004
By PETER PORCO

Ray Dushkin Jr. bent over to pick up a hatch on the deck of his grandfather's fishing boat. The next thing the 19-year-old knew, he was flying backward over the low railing and into the harbor at King Cove near the tip of the Alaska Peninsula.

A sea lion about 12 feet long and 1,200 to 1,500 pounds had leaped out of the water, chomped into the seat of his britches and yanked backward, pulling him under the water, Dushkin said.

It happened in a single swift motion, like the snap of a whip. "One shot," the victim said by phone Wednesday afternoon. "It happened so fast, I forgot what I was doing."

Dushkin spent a few moments beneath the surface before the animal let go, but he was not seriously injured. His left buttock sports an inch-and-a-half scrape, but no bite mark, he said. His coveralls were torn through, as were the pants worn beneath them. And he got a heck of a scare. …

Dushkin, his father, Ray Dushkin Sr., and crew members Charles Mack and Henry Roehl had returned to King Cove on Monday from cod fishing, father and son said. …

"He went over like a rag doll," the father said. "He was off his feet, and in a split second he was under the water." The father was horrified. …

"The only thing I was thinking is, that sea lion was taking off with my boy, and I'll never see him again."

britches: *pants*

Male sea lions can swim faster and deeper than female sea lions.

Quick Fact

Male sea lions don't eat during the breeding season. They care more about protecting their territory.

Creatures are often most dangerous when they are hungry or protecting their young. What do you care about so much that you would fight for it or give up something important for it?

A sea lion leaped out of the water and pulled Ray Dushkin Jr. into the harbor at King Cove.

The Expert Says…

"Feeding sea lions is dangerous to both the sea lions and the public and is against the law. Once sea lions associate humans with food, they are hard to deter from seeking interaction with humans and can become quite aggressive.

— Kevin Heck, Assistant Special Agent-in-Charge, National Oceanic & Atmospheric Administration

Take Note

The sea lion can be a big bully and a dangerous enemy — it can attack other sea creatures and even humans because of its territorial nature. But no one expects this to happen because the sea lion does not appear very threatening, which is why this creature roars in at #10 on our list.
- What are some other sea creatures that have made deadly attacks even though they are not usually known to be dangerous?

9 STINGRAY

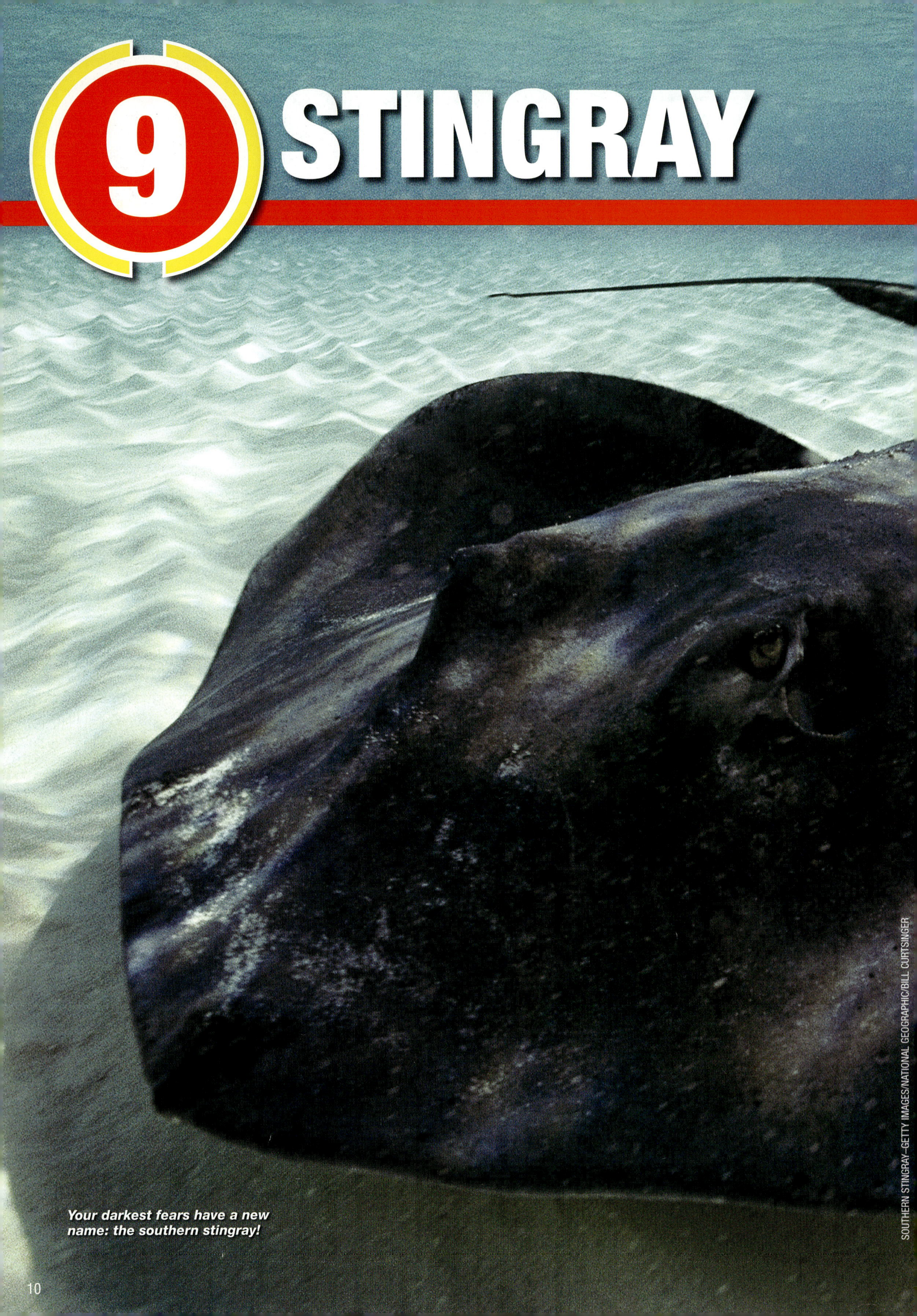

Your darkest fears have a new name: the southern stingray!

SOUTHERN STINGRAY–GETTY IMAGES/NATIONAL GEOGRAPHIC/BILL CURTSINGER

It's hard to believe that you can get an ugly looking wound from one of these beautiful creatures. You may be able to interact with them at vacation resorts, but that's only because vacationers have to be patient and let the stingrays come to them. When stingrays are cornered by snorkelers and divers, look out! Stingrays will use their long, sharp tails to slash and sting anyone who comes too close.

A stingray wound can be very painful, thanks to the venom-filled mucus injected during the sting. Oh yeah, there's also the possibility the stinger could break off and get stuck under your flesh.

Each year, over 1,500 people are injured by stingrays. Most injuries happen when beachgoers accidentally step on the stingrays. There are even cases where people have died from stingray wounds to the chest or neck. Since 1969, 17 people have died from stingray attacks. The stingray-attack death rate is low in human beings, but this sea creature has made it onto our list because of its unpredictable behavior.

What makes some stingray injuries deadly?

STINGRAY

HOME SWEET HOME

Most rays live in the warm shallow areas of the Atlantic, Pacific, and Indian Oceans. There are also freshwater stingrays, which can be found in Africa, Asia, and parts of the U.S.

IF LOOKS COULD KILL

Picture a shark that's been run over by a truck and that's kind of what a stingray looks like. This makes sense because the 100 different types of stingray are related to sharks. Most rays are either oval or diamond-shaped, depending on the pectoral fins they use to "fly" gracefully through the water.

FOOD FOR THOUGHT

The sandy-brown color of most rays is great camouflage while they dig into the sand for crabs, shrimp, clams, fish, and worms to eat. Stingray mouths are located on their bellies, which makes it really easy to eat critters crawling on the ocean floor!

BUT WHAT DOES IT DO?

Stingrays usually spend most of their time swimming or hanging out on the seafloor with their tails and eyes visible above the sand. Although stingrays are able to inflict a lot of pain, they only attack when they feel threatened. When stingrays attack people, they swing their stingers at them. This can cause major wounds, bleeding, and damage to the muscles.

Grey stingray — its venom can stop the heart of a small dog!

Quick Fact

Steve Irwin, also known as the "Crocodile Hunter," was killed by a stingray in September 2006. He was swimming above the ray when its tail flew up and struck him in the chest. Although Irwin was able to remove the stinger, he died almost immediately — the stingray venom had stopped his heart.

Quick Fact

Don't pee on the sting! Some people believe this will help "clean" the wound and stop the pain, but it could make it worse. Doctors recommend flushing out the wound with seawater instead.

The Expert Says...

When a stingray strikes, it either removes its barb entirely, or breaks it off inside of the victim. When this occurs, doctors must probe the wound to make sure all particles have been removed, so the injury will not result in gangrene.

— Dr. Bob Shipp, University of Alabama

gangrene: *death of tissue due to lack of blood*

A stingray camouflaged and concealed from its enemy

Lord of the Stings!

Say you are on vacation, walking through the water, when suddenly — *OW!* You are doubled over in the worst pain. Here's a list of what goes down when you step on a stingray:

- In less than a second, the long tail whips up and sinks up to four stingers into your flesh (these stingers can be from one to four inches long).

- Each of the four stingers has jagged, spiky barbs that pierce the skin easily, but are really difficult and painful to remove.

- Each of the spiky barbs is attached to venom glands, which shoot a poisonous mucus deep into the wound.

- Bacteria are forced into the wound at this time (this often causes pus to develop).

- The wound may bleed a lot, making it hard to remove the bits of stinger left under your skin.

- The venom destroys fat and muscle, causing the area to swell.

- Symptoms such as fainting, nausea, vomiting, and diarrhea start to develop. In rare cases the sting can cause paralysis, seizures, and death.

The Stingray Shuffle

It may sound like some sort of funky dance, but the stingray shuffle could save you a lot of pain. Aside from wearing special equipment or not going in the water, there really isn't any other way to avoid an agonizing sting. But by sliding and shuffling their feet, swimmers can scare away the rays that may be buried in shallow waters near the shore.

Southern stingray

Take Note

Like the sea lion, a stingray's attack is usually unexpected. The stingray's deadliness depends on where the victim is stung. In most cases, a stingray attack is extremely painful, but not deadly. The stingray comes in at #9 on our list because death is almost guaranteed if the barb gets you in the throat or chest.
- Do some research on jellyfish. What are the similarities and differences between jellyfish and stingrays?

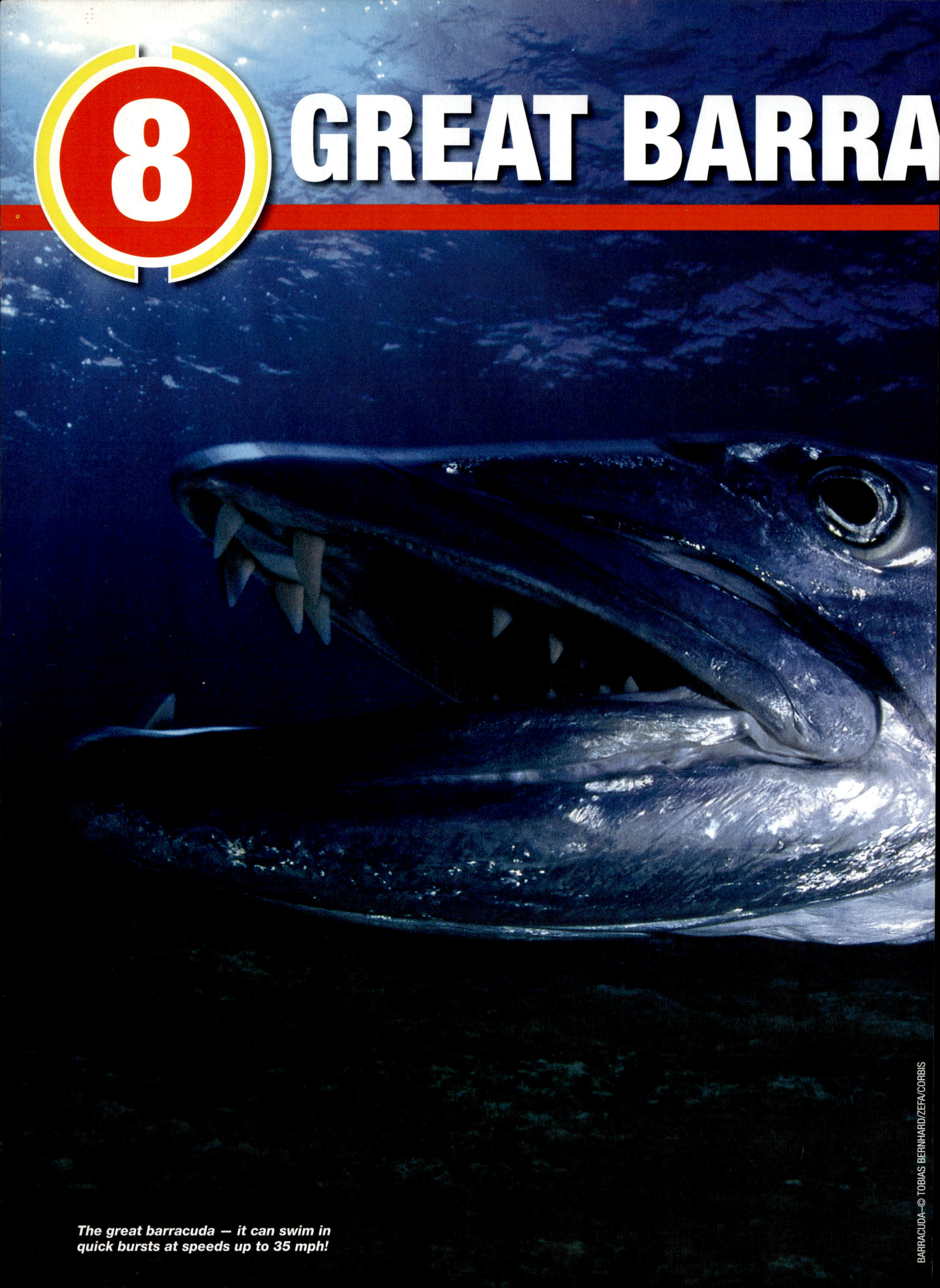

The great barracuda — it can swim in
quick bursts at speeds up to 35 mph!

CUDA

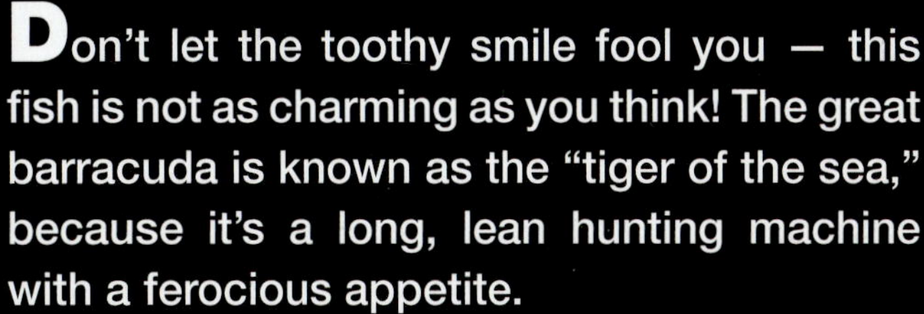

Don't let the toothy smile fool you — this fish is not as charming as you think! The great barracuda is known as the "tiger of the sea," because it's a long, lean hunting machine with a ferocious appetite.

This ocean hunter doesn't just have the body of a killer — it has the attitude, too! The great barracuda is a triple-threat combination of super-fast swimming ability, a fearless personality, and a whole bunch of teeth. It is known to attack swimmers — and the results aren't pretty! The bite of a great barracuda can easily sever arteries or veins, causing some victims to die from blood loss.

BARRACUDA

HOME SWEET HOME

The great barracuda is found in the western Atlantic Ocean from Florida to Brazil. It can also be found in the Caribbean Sea, the Gulf of Mexico, and the Indian and Pacific Oceans.

IF LOOKS COULD KILL

This body was built to hunt! With excellent eyesight, the barracuda can spot the smallest fish even in murky water. It then speeds toward the prey (its narrow body helps it swim fast). The barracuda then attacks with a major mouthful of dagger-like chompers — two sets, in fact.

Quick Fact

Leave the bling at home! Barracuda are attracted to anything shiny, especially flashy jewelry — to them it looks like a small fish. You don't want them taking a bite of you because they think your favorite bracelet is dinner.

FOOD FOR THOUGHT

With a huge appetite, a gigantic mouth, and sharp teeth, the barracuda never has to worry about where its next meal is coming from. Its diet consists of small and medium-sized fish such as tuna, anchovies, pufferfish, and parrotfish. The barracuda has a special hinge on its upper jaw that lets it open its mouth extra wide — making it that much easier to bite you!

BUT WHAT DOES IT DO?

The great barracuda spends its days cruising the coral reefs and looking for victims — er, food. It is brave and curious (most fish aren't), and it often follows snorkelers or divers. Most attacks on humans happen when the barracuda tries to steal speared fish from divers.

? How many types of barracuda are there? How are they different from each other? Research and find out.

The Expert Says…

"Attacks on humans by barracuda appear to be much more common than previously thought; and unprovoked barracuda attacks do occur. I lost a finger and the side of a hand to a completely unprovoked barracuda attack."

— Dr. Thomas J. Goreau, president of the Global Coral Reef Alliance

8

A Diver's Story

By Paul Herring

Divers in Honduras are at risk of encountering this deadly creature. Read this personal account to find out why.

One diver needed 31 stitches after two bites from a mouth like this.

I was helping an instructor with a group of five divers on a night dive at Utila, Honduras. The dive had been an uneventful, routine night dive. We worked our way along the sand to shallow water, about 20 feet deep. We had come about five feet off the bottom and were beginning our safety stop. When suddenly — *boom*! I thought I had been hit by a boat.

I sank to the sand. I was bordering on unconsciousness and mentally talking to myself to remain awake. My mask remained on my face, but was flooded and would only clear to the bridge of my nose. It was full of blood and salt water.

Upon surfacing, I asked Jeff, the instructor, what had hit me. He said I had been attacked by a barracuda. Here's what happened: Jeff had the fish in his light and the barracuda was acting very aggressively. As Jeff moved his light off the fish, the animal exploded into my face and mask. The lower jaw struck my regulator, knocking it from my mouth. The upper jaw struck my mask in the area of the corner of my right eye. Teeth from its upper jaw tore through the mask and through my nose, cutting two small arteries. I lost a ton of blood.

The personnel at the first aid station were not able to stop the bleeding. They finally called Jose Guerra, a Cuban doctor, for help. Twenty minutes later, he had most of the arterial bleeding stopped and had sewed me up.

safety stop: *process that helps divers safely surface after a dive*
personnel: *staff*

Quick Fact

A disturbing barracuda attack happened in the 1990s in Kailua-Kona, Hawaii. A barracuda attacked a woman's head because it was attracted to the shiny clips in her hair. She needed surgery to remove the barracuda teeth from her skull.

Take Note

The barracuda comes in at #8 on our list. The barracuda does not have any toxic venom, but it is fast, furious, and fearless — whether it is attacking or defending itself. It has a mouthful of sharp teeth that penetrate right through a diver's gear and into the body.

- Compare the ways to avoid stingray attacks with barracuda attacks.

5   4   3   2   1

7 SEA WASP

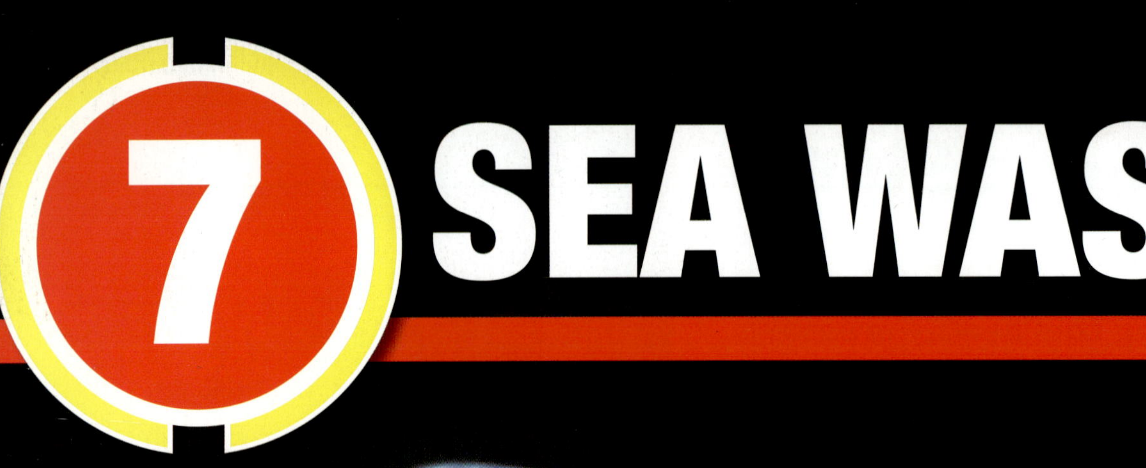

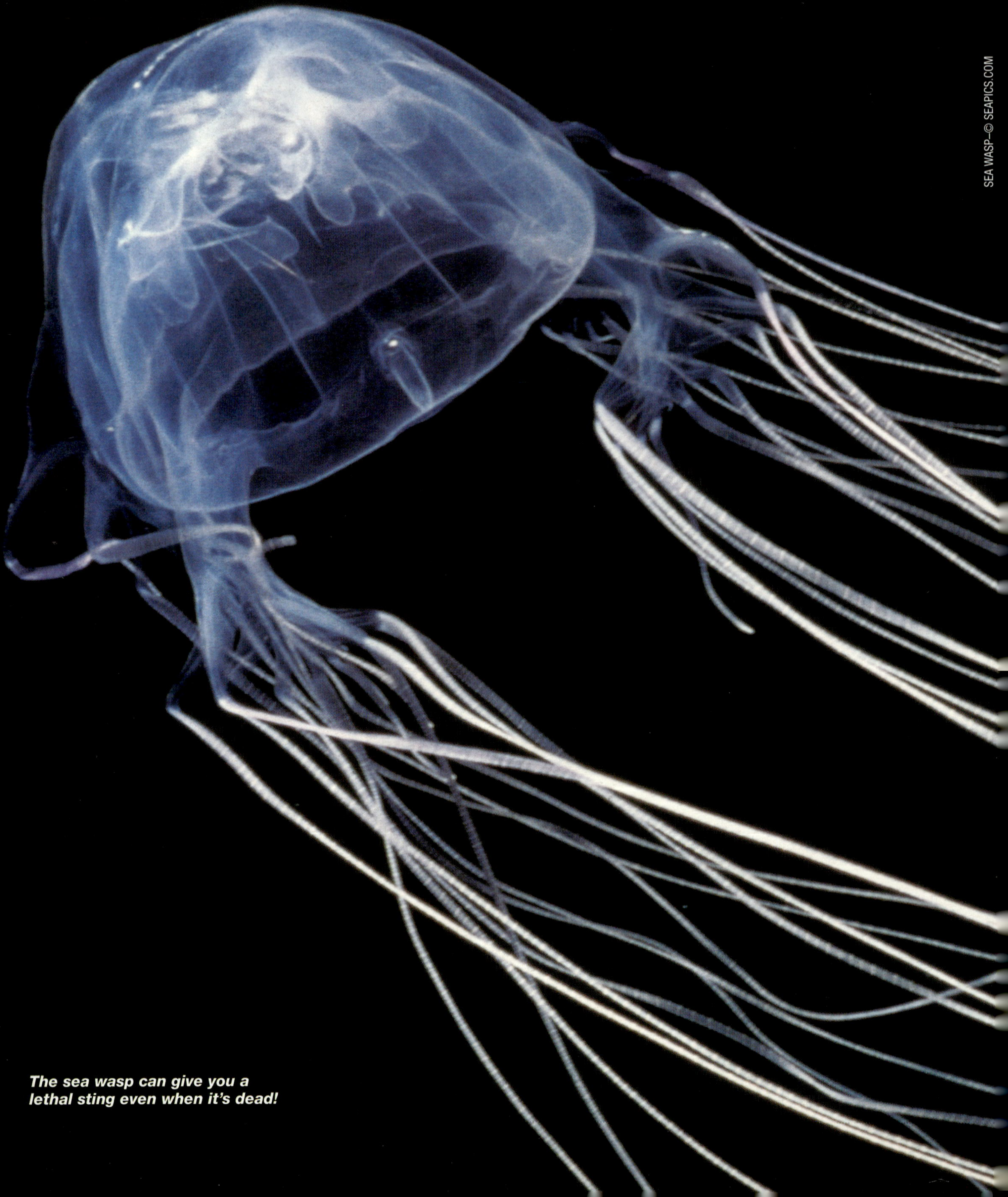

The sea wasp can give you a lethal sting even when it's dead!

Meet the most venomous jellyfish in the ocean! The sea wasp only lives near Australia, and isn't frequently encountered. But if you do meet a sea wasp, you better be careful! A sea wasp's sting can be overwhelming.

The venom in one adult sea wasp is so lethal that it can kill over 50 people. Once stung, you have anywhere between 30 seconds and five minutes to get help, or you could die. The only thing that can save you is antivenom — hopefully there's some nearby!

To make matters worse, these ghostly stingers are hard to see — in clear ocean waters they can be almost invisible. Sea wasps swim underwater at a rate of almost five miles per hour. With their crystal-clear appearances and quickness, it's pretty easy to brush up against one of these sea creatures!

The sea wasp is also known as the box jellyfish. Why do you think the author chose to use the term sea wasp for this book?

SEA WASP

HOME SWEET HOME

Sea wasps are found in the tropical waters of Australia and Southeast Asia. Each year, they kill about 70 people. Most of the deaths happen in northern Australia between November and April.

IF LOOKS COULD KILL

How can something that looks like a floating plastic bag be so deadly? Well, the sea wasp is equipped with deadly venom to help protect its fragile body from predators. The sea wasp's body is sort of bell-shaped with four sides. In Australia, the sea wasp is known as the box jellyfish because its shape resembles a square box. The body of the sea wasp can get as big as a basketball, with up to 60 hanging tentacles dangling down from it. The tentacles can be up to 10 feet long. They are covered in millions of stinging cells that shoot venom into anything they touch.

Quick Fact
Most people who get stung by a sea wasp never even see the tentacles!

The Expert Says...
Jellyfish don't have hands or feet. They have to kill and kill instantly. The venom has a direct effect on the heart and causes immediate death to the tissue it contacts. ... It turns the tissue into soup.

— Jamie Seymour, researcher at James Cook University's Tropical Australia Stinger Research Unit

Quick Fact
Jellyfish are like living blobs. They are only five percent solid, and the rest is all water! They don't even have brains, backbones, hearts, or blood.

The main part of the sea wasp can be as big as a basketball.

FOOD FOR THOUGHT

A sea wasp uses its venomous tentacles to help it catch and eat small fish, shrimp, plankton, and other jellyfish. When a fish gets tangled, the venom kills it almost instantly. This prevents a struggling victim from damaging the sea wasp's delicate body.

BUT WHAT DOES IT DO?

Sea wasps move by sucking in water and squirting it out. Sea wasps are known as "silent stalkers" because they hunt by floating along and waiting for prey to bump into their long dangling tentacles. If they do happen to feel the need for speed, they can also dart along surprisingly quickly.

Why might sea wasps be more dangerous because they are silent stalkers?

7

10   9   8   6

Girl dies after box jellyfish sting

Australian Associated Press, January 9, 2006

Many deaths caused by a sea wasp's venom are preventable. Read the following article to find out how.

A Queensland girl would not have died if she had been wearing protective clothing recommended by authorities to guard against box jellyfish stings, an expert said.

The seven-year-old girl, whose name has not been released, was swimming at Umagico Beach near Bamaga, 25 miles from Cape York Peninsula's most northern point, when she was stung about midday on Sunday.

She was rushed out of the water screaming and collapsed on the beach in front of her parents who quickly called triple 0 [the Australian equivalent of 911].

After a bystander's desperate attempts to revive the girl failed, paramedics arrived and tried to resuscitate her without success. She was taken to Bamaga hospital, where she was pronounced dead at 1:20 PM. Police said tentacle marks across the girl's chest and legs indicated she had been stung by a box jellyfish.

Lisa-Ann Gershwin, national marine stinger adviser with Surf Lifesaving Australia, said the death was an "alarming event" that was entirely preventable. "Even if she had been wearing her mother's pantyhose, or even if she'd been wearing her own pajamas, it would have saved her life," Dr. Gershwin said. "It's a very, very sad thing because this was 100 percent preventable."…

"People have got to understand that these animals are terribly, terribly dangerous — they are the deadliest animal on earth and they can kill you in three minutes," Dr. Gershwin said. "I think maybe we need to have some kind of a roundtable discussion … to just really hammer out how we can approach this so it doesn't happen again." …

resuscitate: *bring back to consciousness*

Quick Fact

If a sea wasp's tentacles come into contact with human skin, they usually leave large brown or purple lines behind that make it look like the victim has been whipped.

Take Note

A sea wasp is not aggressive like the barracuda, but its extremely toxic venom is what puts it at #7 on our list. An attack from a sea wasp means guaranteed death within seconds, but the fact that most of the attacks are preventable is why this ghostly stinger isn't ranked higher.

• Do you agree with the sea wasp's ranking of #7? Explain why or why not.

5   4   3   2   1

6 MORAY EEL

SPOT-HEAD MORAY EEL—SHUTTERSTOCK

Number six on our list is looking pretty fierce! Meet the moray eel, a snake-like sea creature that can do some serious damage.

The moray hides in coral reefs, lashing out if anyone or anything enters its territory. Once it sinks its fangs into you, there's not much you can do. Its bite can cause deep punctures and slash nerves and tendons — it's no surprise that this jagged wound bleeds a lot.

Wait! Things get worse. Sometimes this forceful creature decides to bite down on the victim and won't release its vise-like grip — people have had to kill morays to get them off. Larger morays have even been strong enough to drown people by holding them underwater.

MORAY EEL

HOME SWEET HOME

There are about 200 species of moray eel living in the world's oceans. These bottom dwellers live in the coral reefs, caves, and rocky areas of tropical and subtropical oceans.

IF LOOKS COULD KILL

Open wide! One of the reasons the moray looks so, um, unattractive is because it keeps its big, toothy mouth open constantly so that it can breathe. Speaking of unattractive, the moray is covered in a layer of mucus, which helps it swim and slide through narrow crevices.

The moray's markings help it blend into its surroundings. Because it swims around with its mouth open (that's how it breathes), even this part of the moray is camouflaged.

Golden moray eel

Giant moray eel

FOOD FOR THOUGHT

These excellent hunters usually feed on small fish, octopi, and shellfish. Morays are most active at night, so they have to use their sense of smell to help them hunt. Another helpful feature: moray teeth are perfectly designed for catching moving prey.

? Research other sea creatures. Which ones eat the same kinds of food as the moray eel? Are they just as dangerous as the moray eel?

BUT WHAT DOES IT DO?

Moray eels have been known to attack human beings — mostly when disturbed or provoked. They sleep during the day and don't take too kindly to the hands and feet of curious divers.

Morays have good relationships with certain kinds of shrimp. These little buddies keep the moray looking sharp by eating its dead skin and any parasites on its body. Moray eels can live to be about 30 years old.

The Expert Says…

" … greater respect for moray eels among divers and other ocean users may decrease the likelihood of serious eel encounters. "

— from a case report by Doctors Colin Riordan, Mumtaz Hussain, and Jack McCann

ANYTHING FOR $$$

If you've ever seen an episode of *Fear Factor* then you know that the show's contestants have to do some pretty dangerous and disgusting stunts (which can be fun to watch!). Speaking of dangerous, check out this frightening fact chart, outlining *Fear Factor* appearances made by the moray eel! (Need we say, do not try this at home?)

Yellow moray eel

EEL HELMET STUNT
Episode 93 (Season 5)

Yes, it's as scary as it sounds! In this stunt, contestants had to put their heads in a large fishbowl-like helmet full of moray eels. The goal was to unscrew the bolts that held the water inside the helmet (as quickly as possible) while breathing through a thin tube — and of course — trying not to get bitten!

EEL HANG STUNT
Episode 78 (Season 4)

How would you like to hang out with a tank of slimy morays? For this stunt, contestants were hung upside down over a tank of hungry moray eels. But that's not all — each person had to transfer seven car keys from the eel tank into a bucket. The contestant who did this the fastest was the winner of a new car.

What do you think would have happened to a contestant if he or she had been bitten?

Quick Fact

Talk about lockjaw! Sometimes moray eels just won't let go of a victim. If this happens, the best thing to do is to lure it away with some bait.

Take Note

The moray eel is ugly, slimy, aggressive, and deadly! It is known to bite and not let go of its prey — humans included. The moray eel weighs in at #6 because when it attacks, it can cause serious injuries.
• Any animal that kills is deadly. Would you consider a blue whale, which eats billions of tiny shrimp a year, deadly?

5   4   3   2   1

5 SEA SNAKE

This banded sea snake is deadly in the water, but helpless if washed ashore.

WEIGHT: Up to 10 lb.

LENGTH: 3 to 5 ft.

FEAR FACTOR: Sea snakes have the most powerful venom of all snakes. One drop is enough to kill three humans and up to eight drops can be released with each bite.

If you thought swimming in the ocean was a nice, snake-free activity, you were wrong. Meet the sea snake. It may not be very big or have the largest fangs, but its bite has enough venom to knock out an entire football team!

Think of everything you don't like about regular snakes, and chances are sea snakes have a lot of the same features (except with even more venom!). Keep reading to find out how something with no arms or legs can come in at #5 on our list!

In many opinion polls, snakes top the list of people's worst fears. Why do you think this is?

SEA SNAKE

HOME SWEET HOME

Sea snakes are found in the tropical waters of the western Pacific and Indian Oceans. They are not usually found in the Atlantic Ocean because it is too cold.

IF LOOKS COULD KILL

Sea snakes have up to four small (but sharp!) fangs that can easily penetrate human skin. Once bitten, the venom is released from ducts and injected through the fangs. About 30 minutes after the bite, you'll know something's wrong when you start to experience extreme pain, muscle spasms, breathing trouble, and eventually death.

FOOD FOR THOUGHT

Sea snakes like to eat eels because the long and thin shape slides easily down their throats. They also eat fish and fish eggs. The snake's venom paralyzes prey so that it can eat things that are much larger than it is.

BUT WHAT DOES IT DO?

Since sea snakes have to come up for air, they usually live in shallow water along the shore (and closer to humans!). These curious snakes are usually calm, but watch out during mating season when they can become aggressive. Most sea snake attacks have happened when a diver has disturbed their nesting areas.

Banded sea snake

Quick Fact

Unlike the land snake, the sea snake has a paddle-shaped tail that is used for swimming. It also has valves over its nostrils to keep water out when it swims.

Notice how the snake is equipped to live in oceans. What other air-breathing animals live in oceans?

Quick Fact

Eat or be eaten? In August 2002, Le Hung Cuong, a chef at a gourmet Vietnamese restaurant, died from the bite of a sea snake he was about to cook.

The Expert Says...

" Perhaps the sea snakes are a more advanced form of snake, for only in aquatic animals does leglessness confer an advantage — or at least, it does not handicap the animal. "

— Richard Ellis, author of *Aquagenesis: The Origin and Evolution of Life in the Sea*

confer: *offer; give*

10 9 8 7 6

Meet the Venom Doc

Dr. Fry — moments after he was bitten by this wild python.

Dr. Bryan Fry has milked over 15,000 venomous snakes — all in the name of research! Ever since he could walk, this "Venom Doc" has been fascinated by our slithery friends — especially sea snakes. Dr. Fry and his wife Alexia travel the world collecting and studying the venom of sea snakes. Read this **profile** to find out more:

Olive sea snake

NAME: Dr. Bryan Grieg Fry

UNOFFICIAL TITLE: Venom Doc

OFFICIAL TITLE: Deputy Director Australian Venom Research Unit, University of Melbourne

HE'S A SURVIVOR: Fry has survived 24 venomous snake bites!

FAVORITE SNAKE: "The Stoke's sea snake. Took six years to catch the first one. Then we got at least one a trip, seven trips in a row. Just a matter of finding the right spot."

GEE, THANKS: Fry's research has raised the number of known venomous snakes from around 200 to over 2,000.

HEALING POWER: Studying snake venom and how it has evolved has led Fry to discover some amazing medical breakthroughs. He and his colleagues have identified a strong **anticoagulant** that could possibly be used to treat heart conditions.

WHAT A RUSH! "Working with some of these snakes is the biggest **adrenaline** rush you could ever do. I used to do extreme ski jumping and big-wave surfing, but none of that can touch working with some of these animals."

---

anticoagulant: *substance that can prevent blood from thickening*
adrenaline: *hormone released by the body in response to stress or danger*

Quick Fact

In addition to sea snakes, Dr. Fry also collects venom from king cobras, rattlesnakes, and many other snakes. Snake venom is used to create antivenom, a substance that hopefully can save someone who has been bitten by a venomous creature.

Take Note

The sea snake won't tear at your flesh like a moray eel, but its toxic venom will kill you in about 30 minutes — and it lives close to people. The sea snake has a combination of all the characteristics of the creatures we've ranked thus far — deadly venom, sharp teeth, and contact with humans — which is why it's ranked at #5 on this list.
• Do you agree with this ranking? Why or why not?

5 4 3 2 1

4 STONEFISH

The pink reef stonefish is rare and very poisonous!

WEIGHT: Up to 10 lb.

LENGTH: 14 to 16 in.

FEAR FACTOR: Quite simply, the stonefish is the world's most venomous fish.

If you don't believe the number 13 is unlucky, then you haven't met the stonefish. It may look like a crusty old rock, but the stonefish has 13 sharp spines that can inject you with a super-toxic venom in a split second.

Did we mention that this sneaky fish is also a master of disguise? It is camouflaged to look just like a bumpy rock, so its victims never even know what hit them.

Turn the page for some really good reasons to watch where you step!

STONEFISH

Camouflaged stonefish

HOME SWEET HOME

Stonefish are found in the shallow tropical waters of the Pacific and Indian Oceans, and along the Australian coast. They usually live on stony ocean floors or near coral bottoms.

IF LOOKS COULD KILL

No one said the stonefish was handsome! Instead of scales, it has warty-looking spotted skin covering its entire body. These clumps of skin make it look like a rock with seaweed on it. This helps it blend into its habitat. To top it all off, the stonefish has 13 venomous spikes that are used for protection. These spikes sting any predatory fish or human beings that may harm the stonefish.

FOOD FOR THOUGHT

Here's where the stonefish's camouflage comes in handy. It starts by doing its best impersonation of a rock (staying very still!). Then, when a tasty-looking fish swims by, the stonefish strikes with amazing speed! It also uses this method to hunt crabs and other shellfish.

Quick Fact

High-speed cameras have been used to film the stonefish in action — the whole attack lasts for about 0.015 of a second.

BUT WHAT DOES IT DO?

To avoid being attacked by bottom-feeding predators such as sharks and rays, stonefish often hang out under rocks or ledges. They also bury themselves in the sandy seafloor by using their fins as shovels.

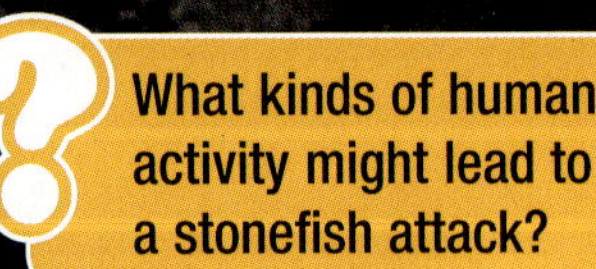

Stonefish

The Expert Says...

"The spines in stonefish are hollow, like a hypodermic needle, and if you stand on the spines, it shoots poison from the venom gland into your foot.

— Dr. Phil Heemstra

"

Anatomy of a Stonefish Attack

Sticks and stones may break your bones, but stepping on a stonefish can be deadly! Check this out this list …

- When weight is put on the spine, the stonefish senses danger.

- It shoots venom through the spine and into the victim.

- The pain is *excruciating* and if the victim is not given antivenom, he or she can die within two hours.

- The sting can also cause extreme swelling and tissue death. Sometimes the victim's limb has to be amputated!

excruciating: very painful

Quick Fact

The spines on a stonefish can pierce through a shoe. If you are attacked by a stonefish, get to a hospital — fast! Wash the sting and soak it in hot water for up to 90 minutes. Don't try to suck the venom out of the wound — it will only make it worse, and could lead to infection.

Take Note

Appearances are deceiving — especially when it comes to the stonefish. It is ranked at #4 on our list because it can easily blend into its surroundings making it a hidden danger. And it has venom that can kill you if you don't get any antivenom within two hours.
- The stonefish is known for its high-speed attacks. How does this add to its other dangerous qualities?

5   **4**   3   2   1

Watch out — if a saltwater crocodile hisses, it's giving you a warning.

OCODILE

Crocodiles, alligators, and caimans are all members of the crocodilian family. But this saltwater croc is both the largest crocodile and the largest reptile in the world!

You can run but you can't hide! Saltwater crocs are fast and powerful. They have been known to attack small boats. They can also attack on land and run quite fast (12 mph).

Watch out! Saltwater crocs can pop up in eastern India, Southeast Asia, and northern Australia and are dangerous to everyone around them!

Turn the page to find out why they are #3 on our list of dangerous sea creatures.

HOME SWEET HOME

You can find saltwater crocs in the coastal ocean waters or freshwater rivers and swamps — between northern Australia and southern India.

IF LOOKS COULD KILL

Saltwater crocs are the world's largest living reptiles. They have between 64 and 68 cone-shaped teeth set inside their powerful jaws. When saltwater crocodiles are young, they are pale yellow with black stripes. As they get older, they become darker in color.

Quick Fact

Hunters found the body of a local woman, two goats, and half a donkey inside a dead Nile crocodile.

FOOD FOR THOUGHT

Make no mistake, these crocs like their meat! When they are young, they eat small mammals, insects, shellfish, and fish. When they get older, they eat snakes, water buffalo, cattle, and pretty much anything else they can sink their teeth into — including humans!

BUT WHAT DOES IT DO?

These crocs like to hunt in the water. They swim slowly toward unsuspecting prey and once they're within reach, they snap open their powerful jaws lightning fast! Sometimes they'll drown their victims. When they prey on large animals, crocs will roll over and over in the water while holding tight with their jaws. This rips up, kills, and breaks victims into pieces for easy swallowing.

A saltwater croc can hold its breath underwater for up to five hours!

The Expert Says...

"Once a crocodile rolls with your arm, leg or whatever in its mouth, you can usually say goodbye to that body part. Those bitten by crocodiles have escaped from their deadly embrace by hitting the head, nostrils and sensitive ears, and poking their eyes."

— Dr. Adam Britton, crocodile researcher

How would the expert's advice help you defend yourself from the creatures you have read about so far?

Myth!

It is often said that you can escape from a crocodile by running in a zigzag way. This isn't true! Human beings can outrun crocodiles on land, and a straight line is the fastest way of putting distance between yourself and the crocodile. Most victims never see the crocodile coming — crocodiles use surprise, not speed.

Maybe you can outrun a croc, but don't get too close to one. If you are within one body length, the saltwater croc can snap into action and grab you before you can even think about moving.

? Saltwater crocs use surprise, not speed, to catch prey. Name two other animals that use this hunting method.

Fatal Attack!

During World War II, a Japanese army unit was fighting on the Burmese Island of Ramree. Being shelled by British Navy ships, the Japanese decided to cross 10 miles of a mangrove swamp. They would be able to join other Japanese army units on the other side. On February 19, 1945, 1,000 Japanese soldiers entered the swamp, which was home to many 16-foot-long saltwater crocodiles.

On the morning of February 20, only 20 of the Japanese soldiers came out on the other side of the swamp!

Adult saltwater crocs have up to 68 teeth!

Take Note

This predator is ranked at #3 because it is a dual threat in the water and on land! It doesn't have any venom, but it does have a huge mouthful of teeth and it can run and swim very quickly. Death by poisoning is extremely painful. However, it seems much more horrific to be torn apart and eaten. Unlike stingrays, these crocs aren't defending themselves when they attack; rather, they want their victims to be their food!
• Which other creatures on the list can commit brutal attacks?

The blue-ringed octopus — its venom is 10,000 times stronger than cyanide, a deadly poison.

OCTOPUS

Something that's the size of a golf ball may not sound like your worst nightmare. Add a sharp beak and enough venom to kill 10 humans and that's when things start to get a little scary …

Say hello to the blue-ringed octopus. This tiny terror doesn't look very exciting — at least until the blue rings light up. Too bad this eight-legged creature is at its most beautiful just before it attacks. If you see the glowing blue rings, chances are it's too late!

HOME SWEET HOME

Blue-ringed octopi can be found in warm, shallow reefs off the coast of Australia and in the Indian and Pacific Oceans. After a storm, it is common to see them washed up on the shore.

How many of the creatures you have read about so far live in or around coral reefs? Why do you think this is?

IF LOOKS COULD KILL

Check out this sneaky stealth feature: when resting, the blue-ringed octopus is a boring brownish color that blends into the reef. It lights up only when it is disturbed (and this is usually the last thing the victim sees before it dies from the venomous saliva!).

FOOD FOR THOUGHT

When you are one of the deadliest creatures in the sea, it doesn't matter if your dinner happens to be a lot larger than you are. The blue-ringed octopus hunts by grabbing and biting prey and then spitting venom into the wound. Sometimes it just spits the venom into the water, paralyzing its victims, usually crabs, clams, and shrimp. The blue-ringed octopus can bite through clothing with its sharp, parrot-like beak.

BUT WHAT DOES IT DO?

When you possess the deadliest venom found in nature, you can pretty much do whatever you want! The sneaky blue-ringed octopus likes to hide in crevices and cracks waiting for unsuspecting prey to crawl past. Sometimes it also hides in tidal pools, which are rocky areas filled with seawater. Many other creatures survive in tidal pools, including dozens of plants, fish, and crabs.

Quick Fact

The blue-ringed octopus's venom comes from two glands — each is as big as its brain!

What does this tell you about this creature?

Close-up of the blue-ringed octopus

The Expert Says...

" There have only been four confirmed deaths in the world ever [from blue-ringed octopus attacks]. In all four cases, people were holding them out of the water. In one case, a [man] was holding it on his shoulder like a pet parrot, poking it and showing his [friends]. It bit straight into his jugular and knocked him out. "

— Dr. Mark Norman, University of Melbourne research scientist and octopus expert

10   9   8   7   6

Eight Things You Didn't Know About the Blue-Ringed Octopus

This list proves that this little creature is not your typical sea dweller.

1 It is used as a murder weapon in the novel *State of Fear* by Michael Crichton.

2 The venom causes muscle paralysis, which means your body loses its ability to breathe and pump blood.

3 Because there is no antivenom, the only thing that can help a victim is artificial respiration.

4 A character in a James Bond movie has a pet blue-ringed octopus that bites one of the bad guys in the face.

5 To eat a crab that it has paralyzed, the blue-ringed octopus breaks through the hard shell with its beak and then sucks out the sweet flesh.

6 Its bite is painless — most victims don't even know they have been bitten.

8 Most males of the species die immediately after mating.

7 Early symptoms of a bite may include numbness, vomiting, blindness, and difficulty swallowing.

Take Note

At first glance it would seem crazy to rank an octopus the size of a golf ball higher than a croc. But when you find out that the blue-ringed octopus has the most toxic venom of all the sea creatures AND there is no antidote, then you might agree with our ranking of #2.

• The blue-ringed octopus lights up before it attacks. What other animals give a warning sign before they attack? Why do you think animals warn people?

5   4   3   **2**   1

Probably not the last thing you want to see before you die.

TE SHARK

WEIGHT: 5,070 to 6,834 lb.

LENGTH: 12 to 20 ft.

FEAR FACTOR: Somehow, a poisonous sting just can't compare to being eaten alive by this cold-blooded killer.

The top spot on our lethal list could only go to a beast known as nature's perfect killing machine.

How exactly did the great white earn this title? Start with its extreme size, add a thirst for blood, super-fast swimming ability, and a starring role in one of Hollywood's scariest films. Still not satisfied? Take a look inside its mouth where you'll see about 3,000 **very sharp** reasons!

If you still need convincing, turn the page for the bloody truth about why this is the undeniable #1 deadliest creature in the sea!

GREAT WHITE SHARK

After a big meal, a great white may not need to eat again for two months!

HOME SWEET HOME

Although great whites have been found in every ocean around the world, they usually avoid the Arctic or the tropics. Great whites prefer temperate waters near the coastlines of Southern Australia, South Africa, South America, and both the western and northeastern U.S.

IF LOOKS COULD KILL

You couldn't invent a better killing machine if you tried! Just look into the great white's mouth — it is three to four feet wide, with row after row of jagged, saw-like teeth. It has extremely well-developed senses (especially when smelling blood). The great white also hunts with unique sensors that can pick up the weak electrical fields given off by all living things. Its gray back and white belly are great camouflage, making it hard to see from above or below.

FOOD FOR THOUGHT

Although famous for eating humans, the great white prefers food with more blubber and less bone. Some of its favorite meals are whales, seals, sea lions, and dolphins. Of course, it isn't too picky and will also eat fish, turtles, and floating dead animals.

BUT WHAT DOES IT DO?

The great white's hunting method involves sneaking underneath its prey and launching a surprise attack. It swims quickly (up to 30 mph) and smashes into the prey (some victims have compared this feeling to getting hit by a car!). The great white then takes a huge bite of the stunned victim and waits for it to bleed to death.

Why do you think the great white would wait for the victim to die before it starts eating?

A great white's tooth can be as big as your hand!

10   9   8   7   6

Quick Fact

A highly-developed sense of smell means that the great white can detect a couple of drops of blood from more than three miles away.

In what ways does this help the great white?

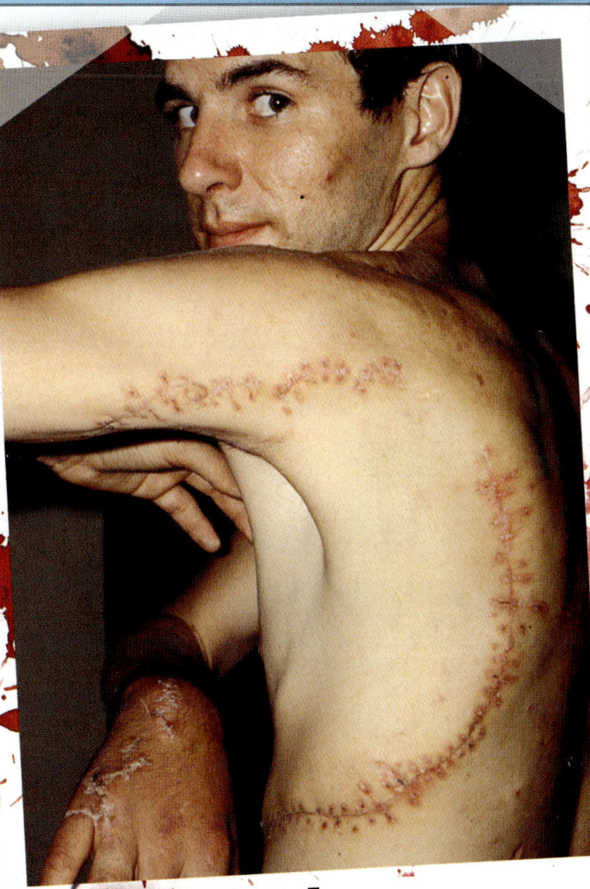

That Bites!

One famous great white victim was Rodney Fox, who needed 462 stitches — his wetsuit was the only thing holding his body together. For some reason he holds no hard feelings toward sharks. Aw, how sweet!

Quick Fact

The great white is sometimes called the garbage can of the sea. Everything from poisonous snakes to license plates, tin cans, old boots, and cardboard boxes have been found inside the stomachs of great white sharks.

The Expert Says...

"It may be a case of mistaken identity or it may be investigatory or territorial behavior. The shark's primary prey are marine mammals, and if you happen to look like one, from a shark's perspective, and you are near the surface, you're at risk."

— Dr. Robert Lea, shark expert for the Department of Fish and Game

Breakfast of Champions

This man shows off a surfboard after a run-in with a shark — not a very healthy meal.

Take Note

Although great white shark attacks are not very common, the great white shark is famous for being a human-eater. An attack by a great white would make a little sting or chomp on the arm look like a walk in the park. All you have to do is imagine how it feels to be eaten alive and you will probably agree with our ranking of #1.

• The fear that surrounds the great white doesn't correspond with the number of fatalities it causes. Why do you think this is?

5   4   3   2   **1**

We Thought …

Here are the criteria we used in ranking the 10 deadliest sea creatures.

The creature:
- Is aggressive
- Is fast
- Looks deceivingly innocent and harmless
- Is camouflaged and difficult to spot
- Has a venomous sting
- Has sharp teeth and a deadly bite
- Lives close to humans
- Has unpredictable behavior

What Do You Think?

1. Do you agree with our ranking? If you don't, try ranking them yourself. Justify your ranking with data from your own research and reasoning. You may refer to our criteria, or you may want to draw up your own list of criteria.

2. Here are three deadly sea creatures we considered but in the end did not include in our top 10 list: Portuguese man of war, scorpion fish, and sea urchin.
   - Find out more about them. Do you think they should have made our list? Give reasons for your response.
   - Are there other sea creatures that you think should have made our list? Explain your choices.

Index